The Grizzly Bear

by Steve Potts

Reading Consultant:
Norm Bishop
Resources Interpreter
Yellowstone National Park

CAPSTONE BOOKS
an imprint of Capstone Press
Mankato, Minnesota

Capstone Books are published by Capstone Press
151 Good Counsel Drive, P.O. Box 669, Mankato, Minnesota 56002
http://www.capstone-press.com

Library of Congress Cataloging-in Publication Data
Potts, Steve, 1956--
    The grizzly bear/by Steve Potts.
    p. cm.--(Wildlife of North America)
    Includes bibliographical references (p.45) and index.
    Summary: Details the life cycle, habits, and behavior of the grizzly bear.
    ISBN 1-56065-469-4
    1. Grizzly bear--Juvenile literature. [1. Grizzly bear. 2. Bears.] I. Title.
II. Series.
QL737.C27P68 1997
599.784--dc21

                                                    96-48684
                                                        CIP
                                                         AC

Photo credits

Visuals Unlimited/Stephen Lang, cover; Tom Ulrich, 30;
    Joe McDonald, 32
William Muñoz, 8, 22, 36
Lynn M. Stone, 6, 10, 14, 17, 18, 20-21, 26, 28, 34, 38-39,
    41, 42
Cheryl Blair, 24

Table of Contents

Pronunciation guides follow difficult words, both in the text and in the Words to Know section in the back of the book.

Fast Facts about Grizzly Bears

Scientific Name: Ursus arctos horriblis (Er-sas ARK-tose HORE-ib-liss)

Height: Average-sized adult grizzlies measure from three to five feet (90 to 150 centimeters) tall when they walk on all fours. When they stand, they measure from six to 10 feet (180 to 300 centimeters) tall.

Weight: Adult grizzlies weigh about 600 pounds (about 270 kilograms). Some have weighed up to 1,400 pounds (630 kilograms).

Physical Features: Grizzlies have a muscular shoulder hump and flat feet. Their claws and teeth are sharp.

Habits: Grizzly bears are loners. They hunt within their own territories. They eat heavily before they hibernate (HYE-ber-nate), which is when they sleep all winter.

Life Span: Grizzlies can live 16 to 18 years.

Color: Grizzlies can have brown, blonde, or black fur. The tips of the hair are gray.

Food: Grizzly bears are omnivores (om-NUH-vors). This means they eat both meat and plants.

Reproduction: Grizzlies mate in June. Cubs are born during the winter while the female grizzly hibernates.

Range: About 40,000 to 50,000 grizzlies live in the mountains, forests, and prairies of Alaska and Canada. Another 600 to 800 grizzlies live in Montana, Washington, Wyoming, and Idaho.

Habitat: Grizzlies live in wilderness areas.

State Animal: The grizzly bear is the state animal for California and Montana.

Chapter 1

The Grizzly Bear

The grizzly bear is one of eight species (SPEE-sheez) of bears found in the world. A species is a group of animals with similar characteristics. Three species of bears live in North America. They are the polar bear, the American black bear, and the grizzly.

The grizzly received its name because of the lighter-colored hair on its back and shoulders. Grizzlies may have brown, blonde, or black fur. But all grizzlies have white or silver coloring on the tips of their fur. This silver coloring makes their fur look grizzled. Grizzled means

The grizzly bear has lighter-colored hair on its back and shoulders.

Adult grizzlies weigh about 600 pounds (270 kilograms). Some weigh up to 1,400 pounds (630 kilograms).

grayed hair. Grizzlies also have thick fur that protects them from moisture and cold.

Size

Grizzlies measure only about three to five feet (90 to 150 centimeters) tall when they are walking on all four legs. When they stand, they measure about six to 10 feet (180 to 300 centimeters) tall. Most adult grizzly bears weigh about 600 pounds (270 kilograms). Some can weigh up to 1,400 pounds (630 kilograms).

Grizzlies' claws are about four inches (10 centimeters) long. Their teeth are about three inches (seven and one-half centimeters) long. Grizzlies have huge back and shoulder muscles. Sometimes a grizzly's big muscles look like a hump on its back.

A grizzly's sight, smell, and hearing are much better than a human's. Unlike a human, a grizzly's senses work equally well during the day or night.

Some people think grizzlies are slow, clumsy animals because of their huge bodies. But they are some of the fastest mammals in North America. A mammal is a warm-blooded animal with a backbone. Grizzlies can run up to 35 miles (56 kilometers) per hour. Few other animals can outrun adult grizzlies.

Plantigrade Feet

Bears have plantigrade (PLAN-ti-grade) feet.
This means that they walk on the entire sole of
the foot.

A grizzly has a heavy pad on the bottom of
each foot. Each foot has five toes. Each toe has
a smaller pad under it.

Grizzlies walk with a
slow shuffle on all four feet.
This way, they can travel
long distances without
stopping. While standing on
their hind legs, they can
only travel short distances.

BEAR TRACKS

FRONT FOOT   BACK FOOT

Grizzlies can travel a long distance when they walk on
all fours.

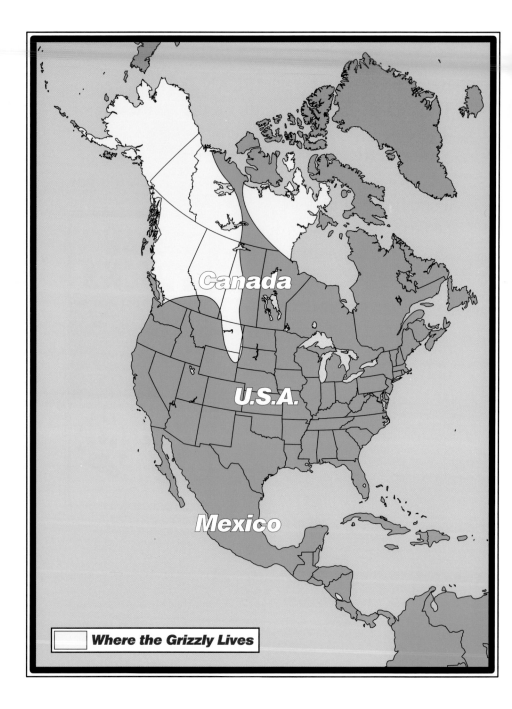

Canada

U.S.A.

Mexico

Where the Grizzly Lives

Chapter 2

Shrinking Territory

Before white settlers came to North America in the 1700s, the grizzly's range stretched from northern Mexico to Canada and into northern Alaska. Grizzlies lived as far east as Ohio and Kentucky.

As settlers moved west, they occupied grizzly territory. The grizzly's food supply became limited. Grizzlies started killing the settler's cattle and sheep. Settlers hunted grizzly bears until they were nearly extinct. Extinct means a type of plant or animal no

Grizzlies prefer to live in mountains, forests, or on prairies.

longer exists. By 1900, grizzlies could be found living in only a few places.

Today, about 40,000 to 50,000 grizzlies live in Alaska and Canada. Another 600 to 800 live in Montana, Wyoming, Washington, and Idaho. Most grizzlies occupy isolated areas far from people. Most people only see grizzlies in zoos.

Grizzlies Need Protection

In the wild, grizzlies live in mountains, forests, or on prairies. Most survive in parks or wildlife refuges (REF-yoo-jez) where they are protected from humans. Refuges are natural settings where animals cannot be hunted.

Sometimes grizzlies leave parks and attack farm and ranch animals. Farmers and ranchers become angry and kill these grizzlies. To prevent such killings, scientists track and medicate the grizzlies. They are then moved to a wildlife refuge away from farm animals.

By protecting them from humans, grizzly bears survive in larger numbers today than other endangered (en-DAYN-jured) species. Endangered means that a type of plant or animal is in danger of dying out.

Scientists study grizzlies by putting radio collars around their necks. Radio collars also help scientists track a grizzly's territory. A territory is an area where animals hunt and roam. By studying the behavior of grizzlies, scientists can help them survive.

Territories

Grizzlies stay in the same territory their entire lives. In these territories, the bears hunt and look for food. The size of a grizzly's territory depends on how much food is in the area.

In coastal Alaska, food is easily available. A grizzly will roam over 10 square miles (26 square kilometers). In other places in North America, food is more difficult to find. Their territory may range up to 300 square miles (780 square kilometers).

Male grizzlies generally hunt in a larger territory than female grizzlies. A larger territory provides more food. Female grizzlies are smaller. They need less food. They must also watch their cubs. Cubs may wander far from their mother. So a female grizzly occupies a smaller territory than a male grizzly.

Grizzly bears like to stay in their own territories. Sometimes grizzlies have been

The size of a grizzly's territory depends on how much food is available in a wilderness area.

trapped and moved far from their home territories. Often they will travel long distances to return to their old territories. Scientists cannot explain how they find their way home.

Grizzlies mark trees to show their territory. They chew or rub the bark off a tree as a sign that they are in the area. A grizzly's territory is

also marked by paths from one food source to another.

What Grizzlies Eat

Many people think that grizzlies eat mostly meat. This is not true. Grizzlies are omnivores (OM-nuh-vorz). Omnivores are animals that eat both plants and meat.

Plants make up about 90 percent of what grizzlies eat. Grizzlies eat grasses, nuts, berries, and roots. They also eat insects.

Grizzlies are good at foraging (FOR-ij-ing) for food. Foraging means to go in search of food. They sniff out honey in beehives. They look for ants under logs. With their powerful legs and shoulders, they can easily smash beehives and overturn logs.

Grizzlies are also good hunters. They usually hunt small animals like gophers and squirrels. They snatch fish like salmon (SAM-uhn) out of streams and rivers. In Yellowstone National Park, grizzlies kill a lot of young elk.

Grizzlies quickly snatch fish out of rivers and streams.

On an average day in the spring and summer, grizzlies eat 25 to 35 pounds (11 to 16 kilograms) of food. In the fall, when grizzlies prepare to hibernate, they may eat up to 100 pounds (45 kilograms) of food each day.

A grizzly will growl and roar if another bear enters its territory.

Grizzlies hunt larger animals when they prepare for winter. Sometimes grizzlies catch and kill weak buffalo, deer, or young elk.

Chapter 3

True Loners

Many animals travel in groups, herds, or packs. The grizzly does not. Grizzly bears like to be left alone.

Grizzlies try to avoid other bears. If adult grizzlies meet, they growl and roar to scare each other away. They stand up, open their mouths, lift their noses, and lay down their ears. They might charge another grizzly to show their anger. Adult male grizzlies will even kill grizzly cubs so their mother might become available as a mate to the male.

Grizzly bears prefer to hunt and live on their own.

Female Grizzlies

Female grizzlies prefer to keep to themselves and protect their cubs. Like male grizzlies, they are usually not friendly to other grizzlies or humans.

Adult female grizzlies, however, are more tolerant of other grizzlies. Sometimes two adult females will travel together. One stays with the cubs while the other one hunts.

Mothers must be tolerant of their cubs. The cubs closely follow their mother's footsteps.

Mating

The one time grizzlies do come together is mating season. Adult grizzlies usually mate in June. Male and female grizzlies stay with each other for only a week or two. Both male and female grizzlies may mate with several other grizzlies during this time.

After the two weeks are over, the males and females go their separate ways. Unlike other animals, grizzlies do not set up families that stay together.

Female grizzlies learn to tolerate their cubs while they teach them to hunt and forage.

Grizzlies and Campers

Grizzlies also try to avoid humans. A grizzly's hearing, eyesight, and smell are keen. Using these strong senses, they can stay out of a human's way.

Sometimes humans and grizzlies meet by accident. Hungry bears will sometimes enter a camp to look for food. They can break open boxes and knock down tents. They might crush cans and packages looking for food.

Campers should not allow grizzlies to find their food. Grizzlies may return to the camp site to find more food. Grizzlies may be killed if they become a problem.

A female grizzly with cubs might think that campers are a threat to her cubs. She may charge and seriously hurt campers. Campers in parks and reserves have been attacked and seriously hurt by grizzlies.

A grizzly's keen senses help it avoid contact with humans.

Chapter 4

Hibernation and Cubs

Grizzlies hibernate (HYE-bur-nate) in winter. Hibernate means to sleep through the winter. Their breathing slows down, and they sleep.

To survive winter, grizzlies eat large amounts of food during summer and fall. They build up a 10-inch (25-centimeter) layer of fat before they hibernate.

New Dens
In late fall, each grizzly prepares its winter home. A grizzly looks for a cave or

To survive winter, grizzlies eat a lot of food .

A cub may grow to weigh 200 pounds (90 kilograms) before it is one year old.

underground hole to use for its den. If it cannot find a cave or underground hole, it digs a den. A grizzly builds a short tunnel and a sleeping hole. It pulls grass, branches, and leaves into the hole to make a bed. A grizzly finds or makes a new den every year.

Females go into hibernation in October or early November. Males wait until the first large snowfall. Then they enter their dens.

Once grizzlies go into hibernation, they sleep for several weeks. They wake up, move around, clean themselves, and push their beds around. Then they go back to sleep. But they do not sleep deeply.

Loud noises will wake up a hibernating grizzly. If a grizzly wakes up, it does not go out to find food. It stays in its den. As a result, a grizzly loses almost 40 percent of its weight by springtime.

Grizzlies will hibernate until late winter or early spring. Scientists do not understand how bears seem to know when to wake up. Still, every spring, grizzlies wake up. They leave their dens and begin searching for food.

Grizzly Cubs

For the female grizzly, waking up from hibernation often means finding new cubs that were born while she slept. Grizzly cubs are usually born in late January. They are small. They weigh about one pound (about half a kilogram) and are one foot (30 centimeters) in length.

During spring and summer, a cub learns how to survive.

A female grizzly usually has twin cubs. But it is not unusual for a female to have between one and four cubs. For three months, the cubs are helpless. They survive by nursing in the den.

Cubs leave the den in spring. They stay close to their mother for several months. They continue nursing until fall. The mother gradually stops nursing her cubs. The cubs may, however, nurse through the next winter.

During their first spring and summer, cubs learn how to survive. For them, this period is like school.

The cubs learn their mother's territory and how to hunt. They also learn which animals to fear and which ones to eat. Cubs may put on 200 pounds (90 kilograms) before they are one year old. Besides hunting for food, a cub spends much of its time running, playing, and learning to climb trees.

Growing Up

Cubs usually stay with their mother until they are three years old. Then the cubs leave their mother. The mother prepares to breed again.

Cubs may stay together for another two years before separating. Then they set up their own territories and begin life as adult grizzlies. They start mating when they are six or seven years old.

The average grizzly lives to be 16 to 18 years old. Some grizzlies have been known to live as long as 30 years.

Chapter 5

Grizzlies and People

Many North American Indian groups tell stories about grizzly bears. The bear is an animal they greatly respect. They believe the bear is an animal full of wisdom, strength, and power.

When Grizzlies Walked Upright

This story is told by the Modoc (MAW-dawk) Indians. They are Plains Indians from the northwestern United States.

The Modoc story says that one day Sky Spirit piled snow from the earth up to a cold

The Modoc Indians tell a story about grizzlies that once walked upright.

sky. This big mound became Mount Shasta. Sky Spirit walked down the mountain. His footprints created streams and trees.

Sky Spirit broke pieces off the small end of his walking stick. He threw them into the river. These pieces turned into small animals such as beaver, otter, and fish.

He used the giant end of the stick to create larger animals. One of those animals was the grizzly bear. At first, the grizzly bear walked upright and talked like humans.

Carried in the Wind

Sky Spirit became tired of the cold sky. He went to live between the peaks of mountains around Mount Shasta. One day, Wind Spirit decided to create a strong wind. Sky Spirit thought it was too strong and too cold.

Sky Spirit sent his daughter to the top of the peak to tell Wind Spirit to lessen the wind. Sky Spirit warned his daughter not to stick her head too far over the peak or she might blow away.

An Indian legend says that grizzlies were cursed and had to walk on all fours.

Shoulder Hump

Snout

Sharp Claws

Grizzled Fur

Darker Underhair

Plantigrade Feet

But Sky Spirit's daughter pushed her head up too far over the peak anyway. She blew away. A family of grizzlies found her and raised her.

She married the oldest grizzly son. They started their own family. The creatures did not look like a grizzly or Sky Spirit's daughter. But the grizzlies were proud of this new breed.

Grizzly Children

The old mother grizzly bear knew that she would die soon. She wanted Sky Spirit to know she had kept his daughter all those years. She sent her youngest grandson up in a cloud to tell Sky Spirit where his daughter was living. Sky Spirit quickly marched down Mount Shasta and found his daughter.

He became angry when he learned that the strange creatures were his grandchildren. A new race had been created without his approval. Sky Spirit then cursed all the grizzlies. From then on, all grizzlies walked on

The legend says that a family of grizzlies raised Sky Spirit's daughter.

Currently, the grizzly bear is an endangered species. People can help save the grizzly and its home.

four feet and never talked again. He took his daughter back to live in the sky.

His grandchildren scattered over the earth. They were the first of all the different Indian nations. This is why the Indians living around Mount Shasta would never kill a grizzly bear.

The Future
In the past 100 years, larger cities and more people have reduced the amount of wilderness land. Grizzlies need wilderness areas to hunt and forage. In the 1850s, about 100,000

grizzlies lived in western North America. By 1900, only about 1,000 grizzlies survived the loss of their natural habitat.

Grizzlies no longer live on the vast western prairies of North America. They remain only in Alaska, the mountains of western Canada, and small parts of Montana, Wyoming, Washington, and Idaho. In California, the grizzly is the state animal. Today no grizzlies can be found in California, however.

Currently, the grizzly bear is an endangered species. People can help save the grizzly and its home. People can build fewer homes, buildings, and highways in wildlife areas. Campers, hikers, and hunters can choose to do outdoor activities in less remote wildlife areas. Grizzlies will then be able to roam freely without the threat of human presence.

Scat, pictured below, is used to find out where an animal lives and what it eats.

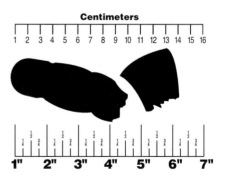

Centimeters
1 2 3 4 5 6 7 8 9 10 11 12 13 14 15 16

1" 2" 3" 4" 5" 6" 7"

Words to Know

endangered (en-DAYN-jured)—a species of plant or animal in danger of dying out

extinct (ek-STINGKT)—a plant or animal that has died out

forage (FOR-ij)—to search for food

hibernate (HYE-bur-nate)—to spend the winter in a deep sleep

legend (LEJ-uhnd)—a story handed down from an earlier time

mammal (MAM-uhl)—a warm-blooded animal with a backbone that nurses its young

omnivore (OM-nuh-vor)—an animal that eats both plants and animals

plantigrade (PLANT-a-grade)—animals that walk on the entire sole of the foot

radio collar (RAY-de-oh KOL-ur)—a collar used to track animals

scat (SKAT)—animal droppings

territory (TER-uh-tor-ee)—an area where animals hunt and roam

To Learn More

Kallen, Stuart A. *Grizzly Bears.* Bears.
Minneapolis: Abdo & Daughters, 1998.

Parker, Janice. *Grizzly Bears.* The Untamed
World. Austin, Texas: Raintree Steck-
Vaughn, 1997.

Silverstein, Alvin. *The Grizzly Bears.*
Endangered in America. Brookfield, Conn.:
Millbrook Press, 1998.

Useful Addresses

Canadian Nature Federation
One Nicholas Street, Suite 520
Ottawa, ON K1N 7B7
Canada

The Craighead Wildlife-Wetlands Institute
5200 Upper Miller Creek Road
Missoula, MT 59803

The Great Bear Foundation
P.O. Box 1289
Bozeman, MT 59715-1289

Yellowstone Grizzly Foundation
104 Hillside Court
Boulder, CO 80302-9452

Internet Sites

The Bear Den
http://www.bearden.org

National Wildlife Foundation—Grizzly Bear
http://www.nwf.org/nwf/wildalive/grizzly

Safety Tips for Travel in Bear Country
http://www.nps.gov/noca/bear.htm

Yellowstone Park Bears
http://www.yellowstone-bearman.com/
    bearman/bears.html

Index